MAGIC EYE II

Now you see it ...

3D Illusions by N.E. Thing Enterprises

PENGUIN BOOKS

PENGUIN BOOKS

Published by the Penguin Group
Penguin Books Ltd, 27 Wrights Lane, London W8 5TZ, England
Penguin Books USA Inc., 375 Hudson Street, New York, New York 10014, USA
Penguin Books Australia Ltd, Ringwood, Victoria, Australia
Penguin Books Canada Ltd, 10 Alcorn Avenue, Toronto, Ontario, Canada M4V 3B2
Penguin Books (NZ) Ltd, 182–190 Wairau Road, Auckland 10, New Zealand

Penguin Books Ltd, Registered Offices: Harmondsworth, Middlesex, England

First published in Great Britain by Michael Joseph 1994
Published in Penguin Books 1995
1 3 5 7 9 10 8 6 4 2

Copyright © N. E. Thing Enterprises, 1994
All rights reserved

Made and printed in Great Britain by William Clowes Ltd, Beccles and London

FOREWORD

As Wizzy Nodwig says, "What you see is NOT what you get!" Wizzy's work can be found almost everywhere these days. MAGIC EYE messages are on the walls of subway stations, or in those silly envelopes they send checks in. If you're a teacher, watch those Pinto notebook covers. If you're a counterspy, give it up, the crazy pinhead might put a message anywhere! (If you're an extraterrestrial . . . welcome!)

With Wizzy's help we've created MAGIC EYE II: *Now You See It* . . . (but it's not what you think!).

Several of the 3D illusions in this new edition require, or at least deserve, a bit of explanation. They may be more difficult to "see," or understand, than the rest. In general this book is NOT presented in the order of ascending difficulty. We continue to believe that the MAGIC EYE technique is a new and challenging medium and our goal is to see it accepted as a valid form of artistic expression.

PAGE 5: Disappearing colors. The 3D item here is a simple cone. The colors of the image are mixed in the brain when viewing the illusion, and "cancel each other out," creating the perception that the picture is in black and white! The colors reappear like magic when you snap back to normal vision!

PAGE 6: Two-Layer Sphere. The 3D item is a transparent sphere. Think of it as being made from two layers of wire mesh, so that you can look at either the front of the sphere or through the front to the back. When looking through to the back layer, the divergence of the eyes causes you to see a different interpretation of the front layer, which will appear to be partially behind the second layer. Trace it back further and . . .

PAGE 27: Two-Layer/Three-Layer. The 3D illusion here has two layers on the top, which weave in and out of each other, and three layers on the bottom, shaped like a wave coming out at you. Can you see them all? Try to divert your eyes further and catch the second overlap. A world that might be nice to fall into.

I want to thank Cheri Smith for her individual work, and to say how much I admire the creations of Andy Paraskevas. They have both worked very hard to create these MAGIC EYE illusions. In addition, thanks to Lynn Door, Dana Finnegan, Iren Rice, Sue Thiebault, Clint Baker, and Eric DeWitt, who are all vital members of the N.E. Thing team —keeping the business running, computers computing, and smiles beaming. Mark Gregoric, who works in the faraway land of New Jersey, has also contributed in many, many ways.

And then, of course, there's Wizzy Nodwig, our resident wizard. Although I've come to respect him more than a little bit, he does babble well over his allotted share. Some have said that although his bulb seems good, his filament is short a few twists. I guess it's true that he's still got a pretty fair piece to go before you could properly call him a Master Wizard, but he's the best we've got here at N.E. Thing, at least for now.

It was Wizzy who once said: "The secret is to find the balance between order and chaos . . . to find your place in the almost symmetry. Life is like a single, beautiful butterfly in a gentle swirling snowstorm. When you find your own center, you'll find the butterfly. Then you can hop on and go on a ride forever!"

Look for his picture on our LOGO!

—TOM BACCEI
JANUARY 1994

VIEWING TECHNIQUES

Learning to use your MAGIC EYE is a bit like learning to ride a bicycle. Once you get it, it gets easier and easier. If possible, try to learn to use your MAGIC EYE in a quiet, meditative time and place. It is difficult for most people to first experience deep vision while otherwise preoccupied in the distracting pinball machine of life. While others teach you, or watch as you try, you're likely to feel foolish and suffer from performance anxiety. Although MAGIC EYE is great fun at work and other entertaining social situations, those are not often the best places to learn. If you don't get it in two or three minutes, wait until another, quieter time. And, if it's hard for you, remember, the brain fairy did not skip your pillow. For most people, it's a real effort to figure out how to use the MAGIC EYE. Almost all of them tell us the effort was well worth it!

In all of the images in MAGIC EYE, you'll note a repeating pattern. In order to "see" a MAGIC EYE picture, two things must happen. First, you must get one eye to look at a point in the image, while the other eye looks at the same point in the next pattern. Second, you must hold your eyes in that position long enough for the marvelous structures in your brain to decode the 3D information that has been coded into the repeating patterns by our computer programs.

There are two methods of viewing our 3D images: Crossing your eyes and diverging your eyes. Crossing your eyes occurs when you aim your eyes at a point between your eyes and an image; diverging your eyes occurs when your eyes are aimed at a point beyond the image.

All of our pictures are designed to be seen by diverging the eyes. It is also possible to see them with the cross-eyed method, but all the depth information comes out backward! (If you try it, we can guarantee that you will not come out backward, too.) If we intend to show an airplane flying in front of a cloud, using the diverging eye method, you will see an airplane-shaped hole cut into the cloud if you look at it with the cross-eyed method. Once you learn one method, try the other. It's fun, but most people do better with one or the other. We think that most people prefer the diverging method.

Another common occurrence is to diverge the eyes twice as far as is needed to see the image. In this case, a weird, more complex version of the intended object is seen. (By the way, if you diverge your eyes while looking at yourself in a mirror, you can find your "third eye" . . . at least we were told that in a letter we received. But you must spend several hours a day looking at yourself in a mirror. Remember, we said it was all right.)

One last note before you start. Although this technique is safe, and even potentially helpful to your eyes, don't overdo it! Straining will not help, and could cause you to feel uncomfortable. That is not the way to proceed. Ask your nephew or the paper girl to give you some help; they'll probably be able to do it in ten seconds. The key is to relax and let the image come to you.

METHOD ONE

Hold the image so that it touches your nose. (Ignore those who might be tempted to make comments about you.) Let the eyes relax, and stare vacantly off into space, as if looking through the image. Relax and become comfortable with the idea of observing the image, without looking at it. When you are relaxed and not crossing your eyes, move the page slowly away from your face. Perhaps an inch every two or three seconds. Keep looking through the page. Stop at a comfortable reading distance and keep staring. The most discipline is needed when something starts to "come in," because at that moment you'll instinctively try to look at the page rather than looking through it. If you look at it, start again.

METHOD TWO

The cover of this book is shiny; hold it in such a way that you can identify a reflection. For example, hold it under an overhead lamp so that it catches its light. Simply look at the object you see reflected, and continue to stare at it with a fixed gaze. After several seconds, you'll perceive depth, followed by the 3D image, which will develop almost like an instant photo!

The last pages of this book provide a key that shows the 3D picture that you'll see when you find and train your MAGIC EYE.

There are some images in the book that do not contain a hidden picture; instead the various repeated objects will seem to float in space at different distances when viewed correctly. These images are on page 8 and 28. For many, they are easier to see than the other pictures.

We wish you luck, and hope you enjoy this fantastic new art form!

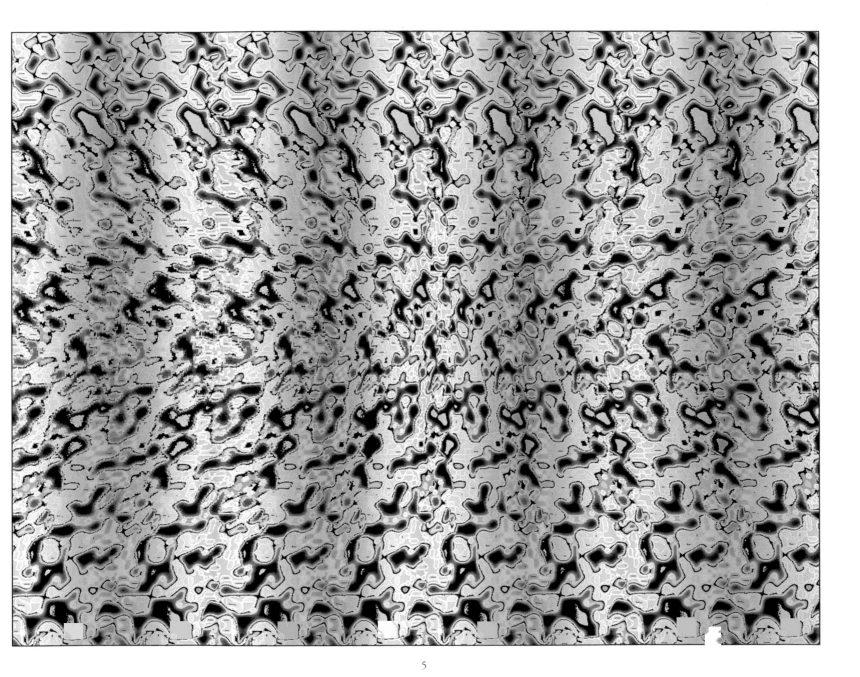

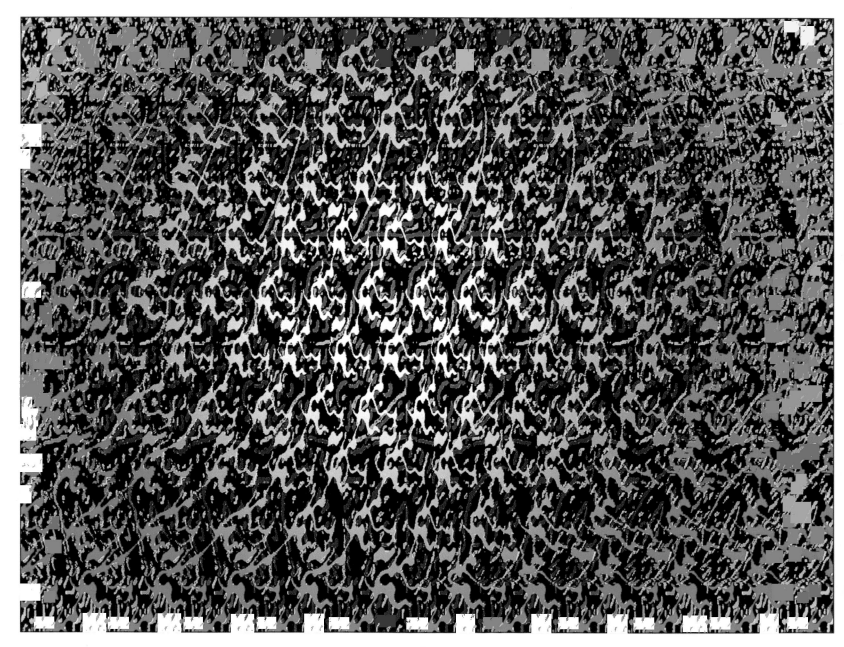

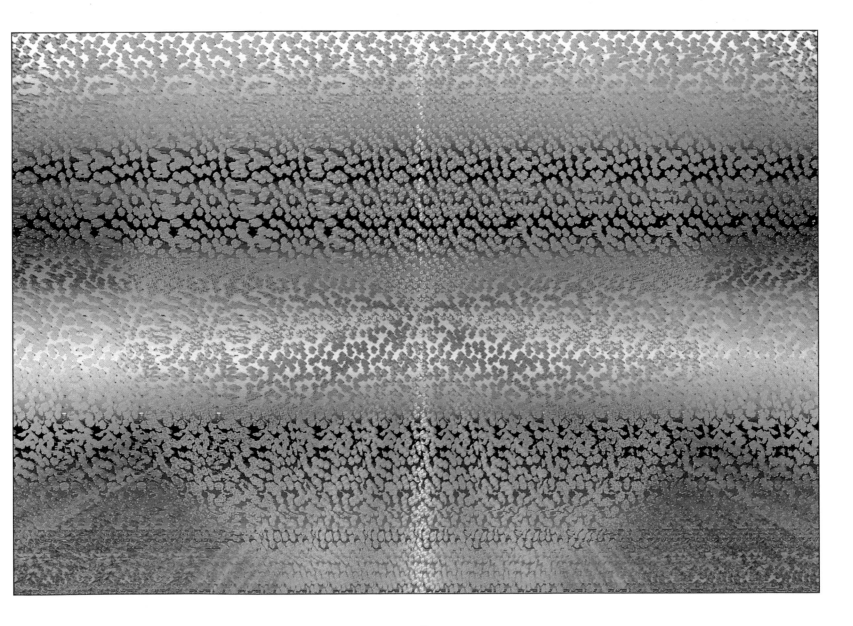

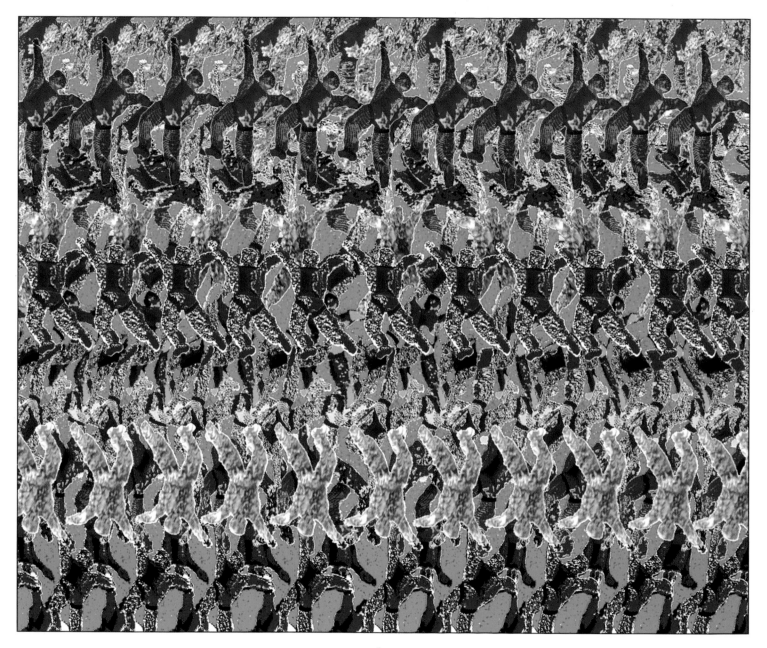

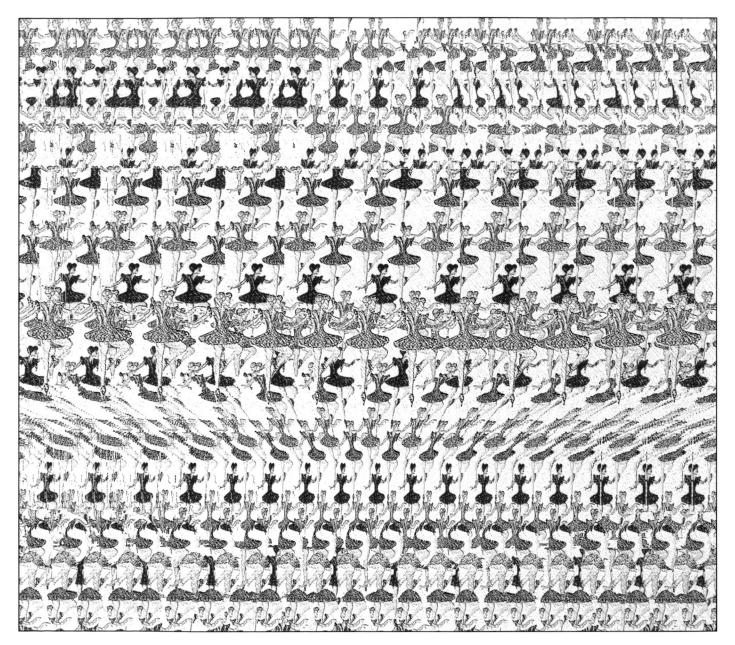

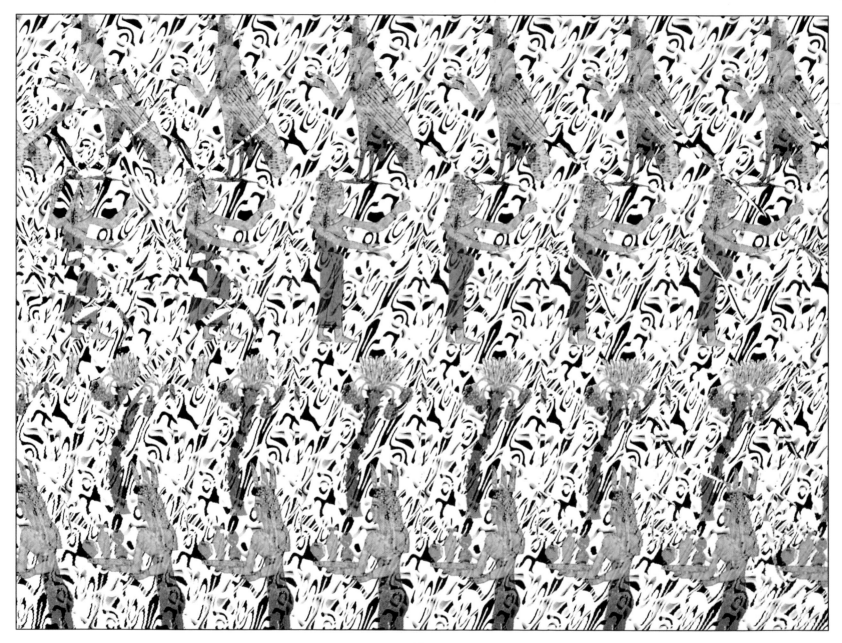

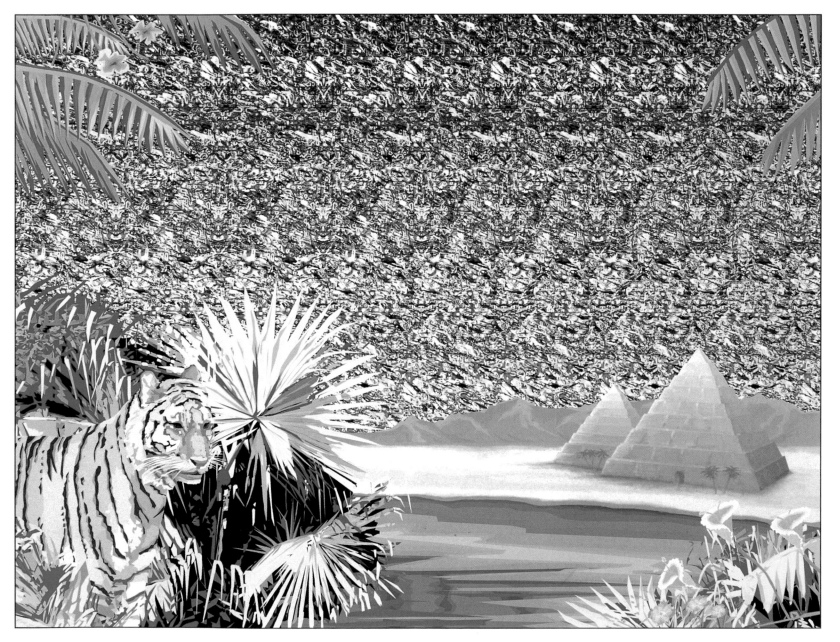

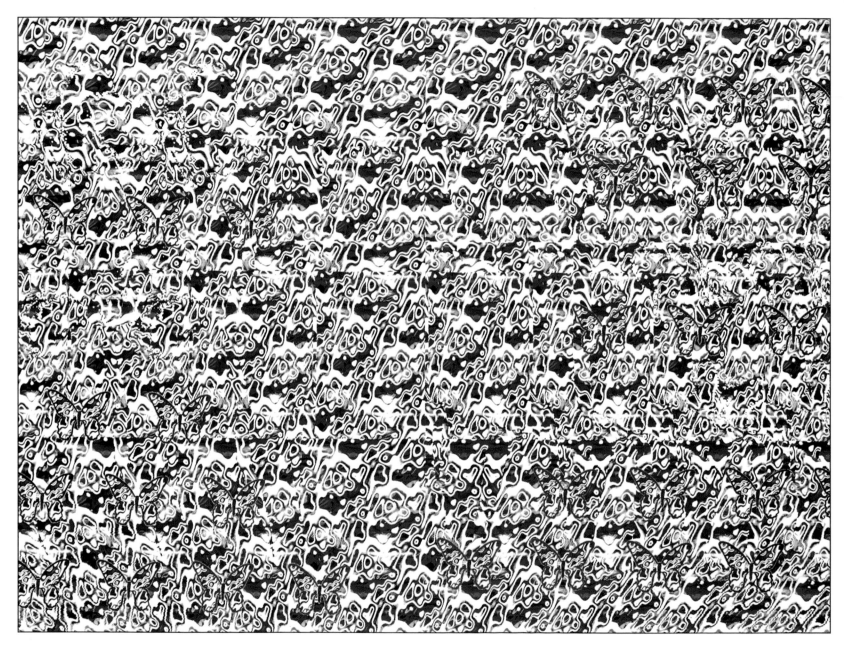

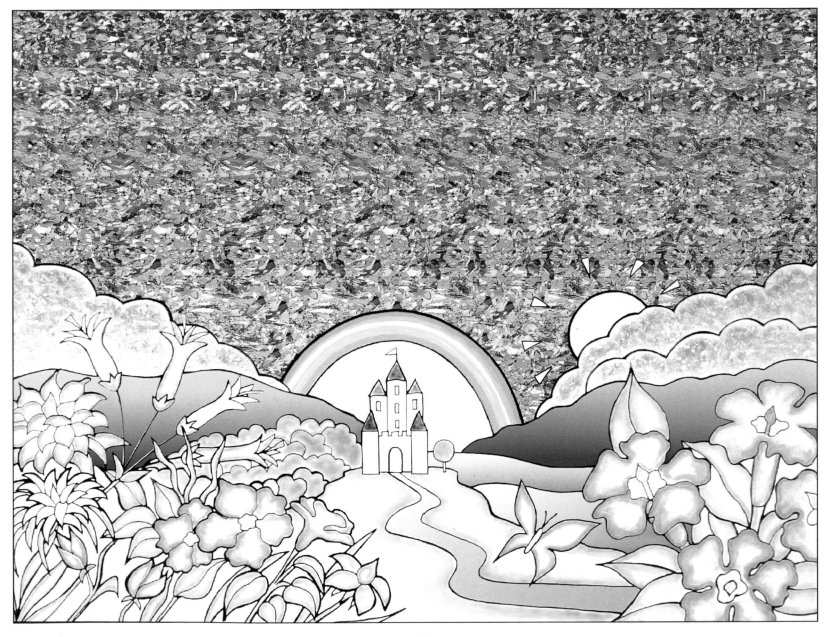

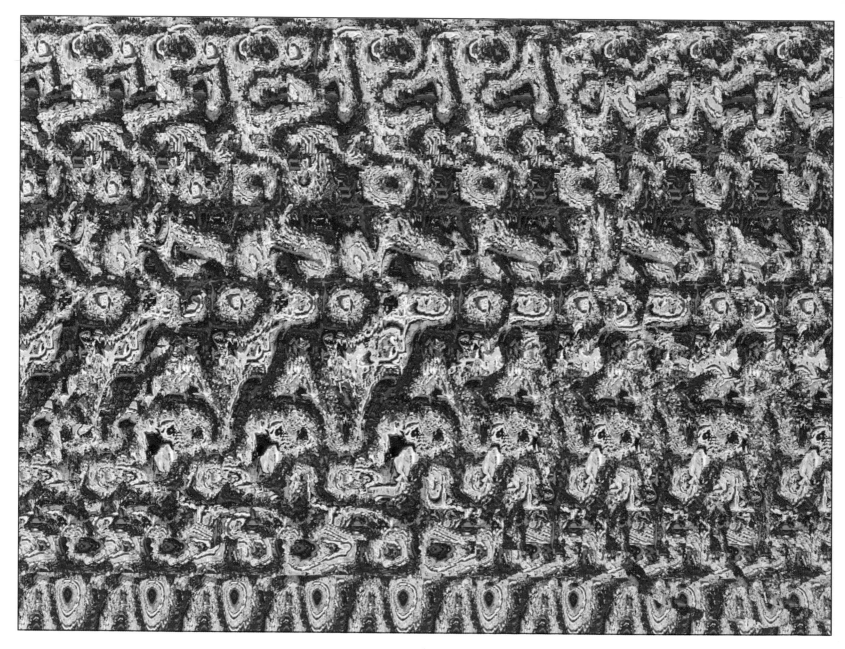

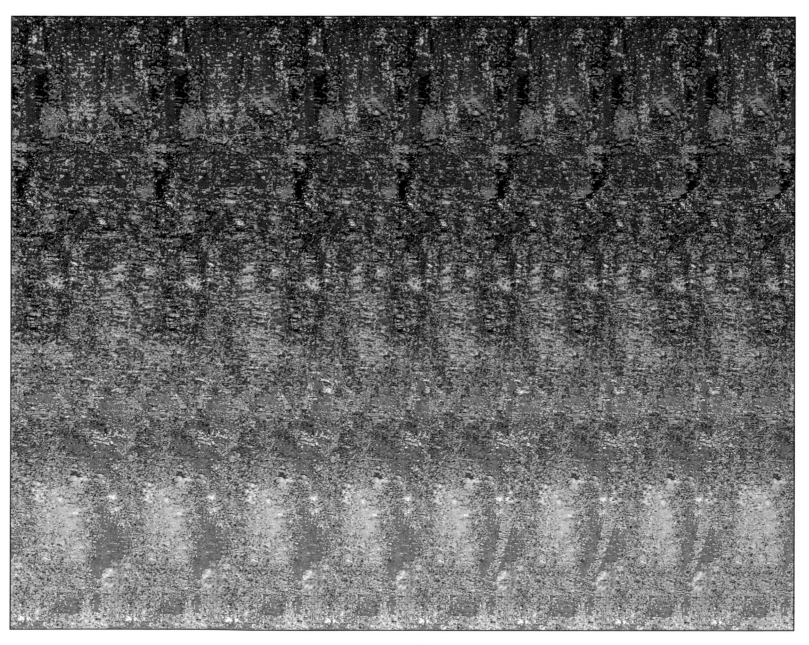

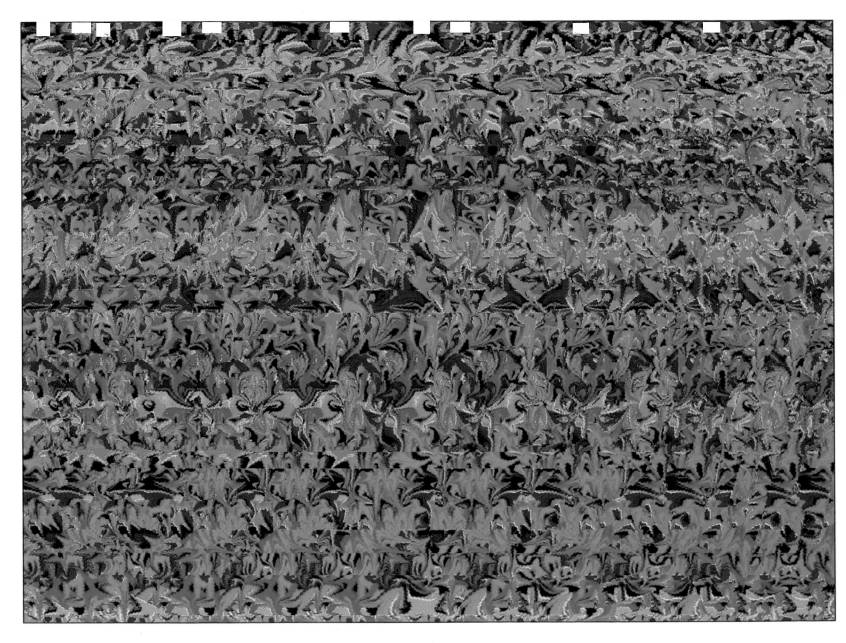

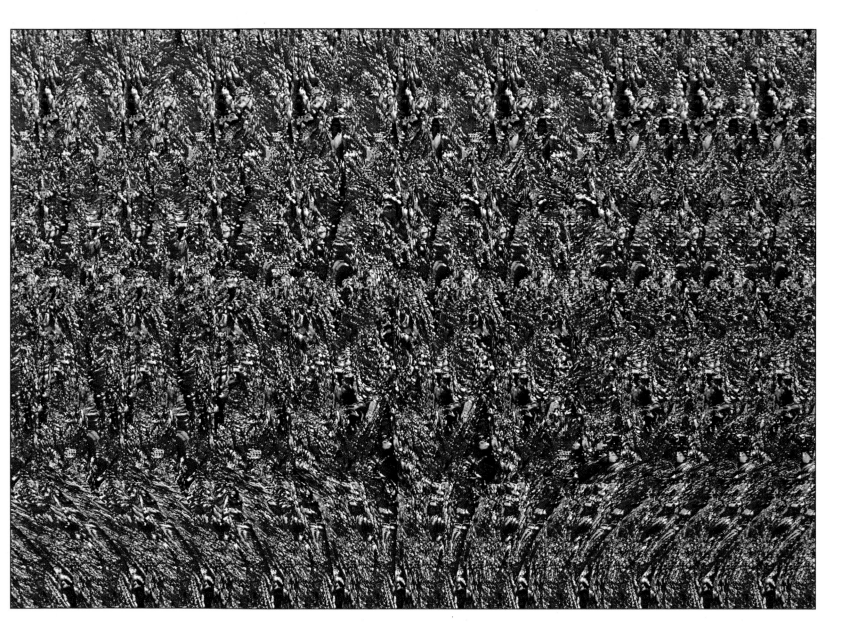

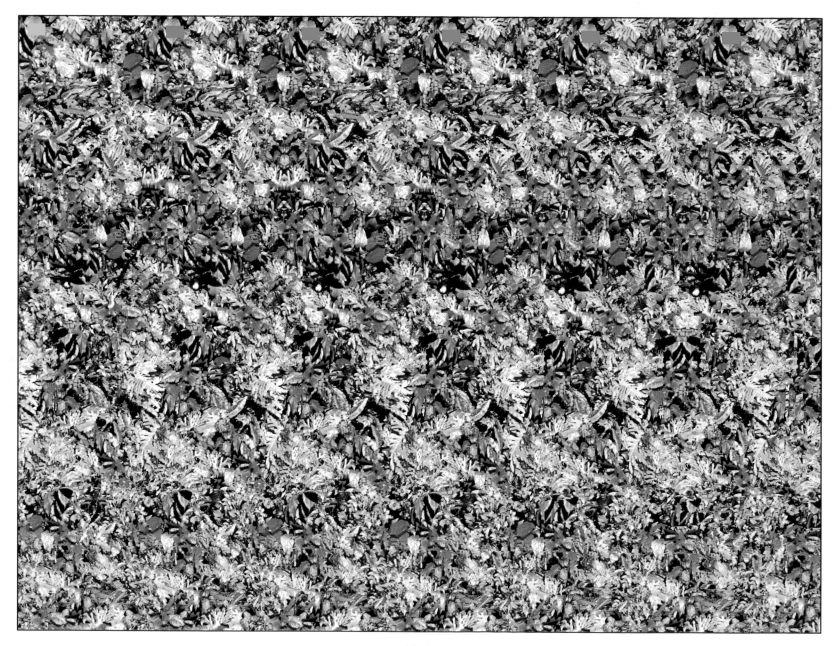

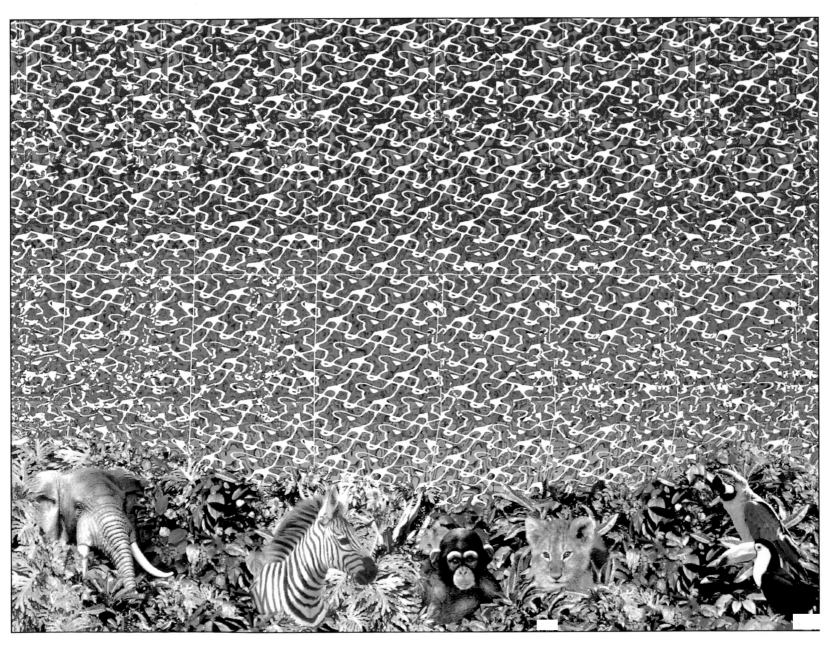

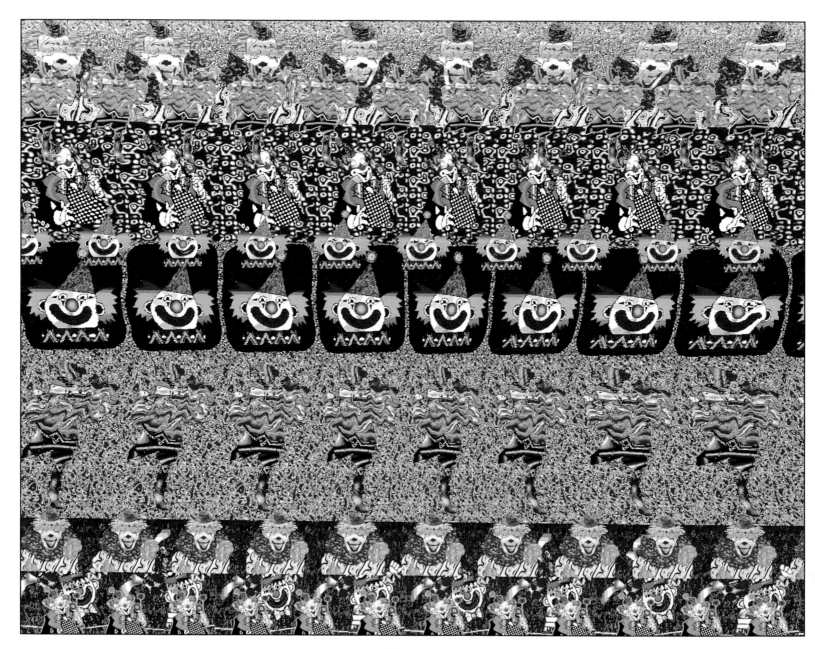

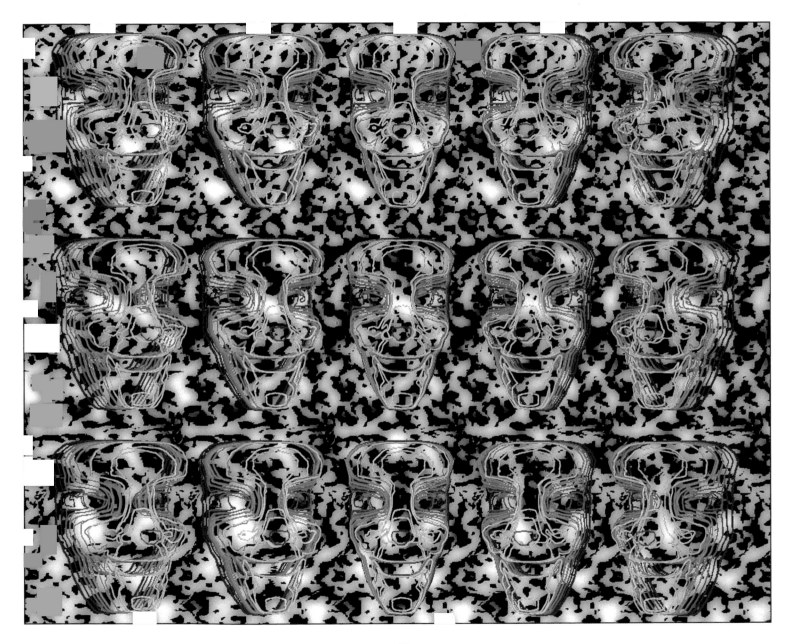

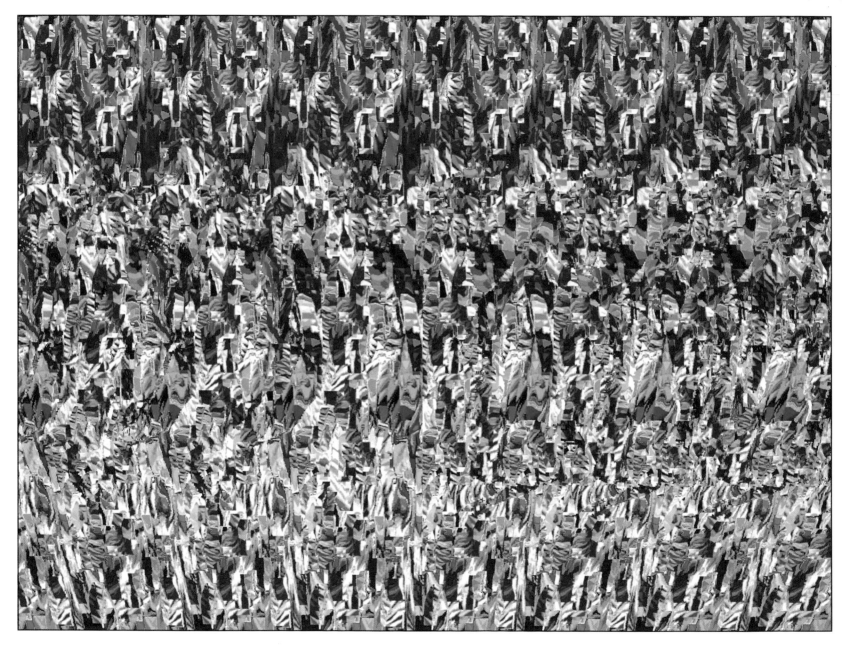

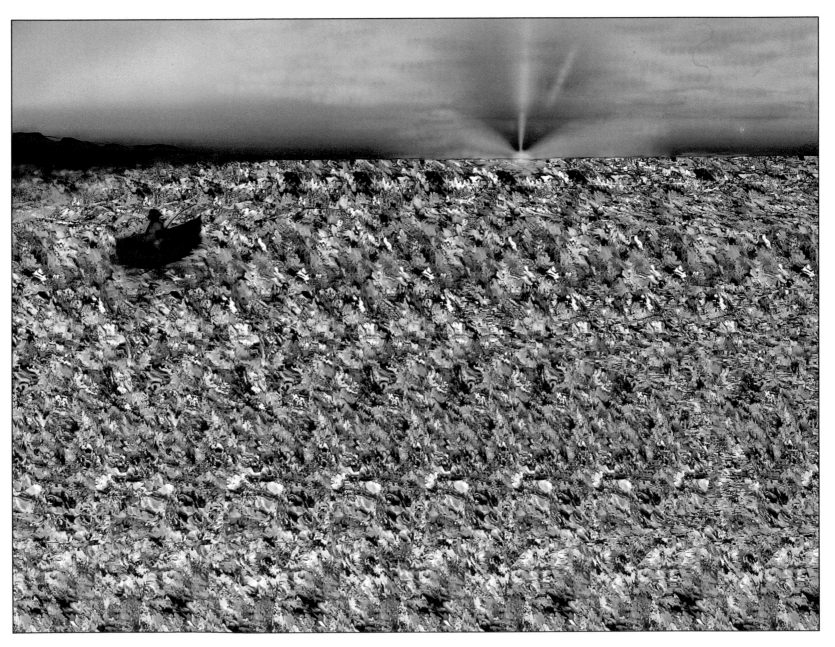

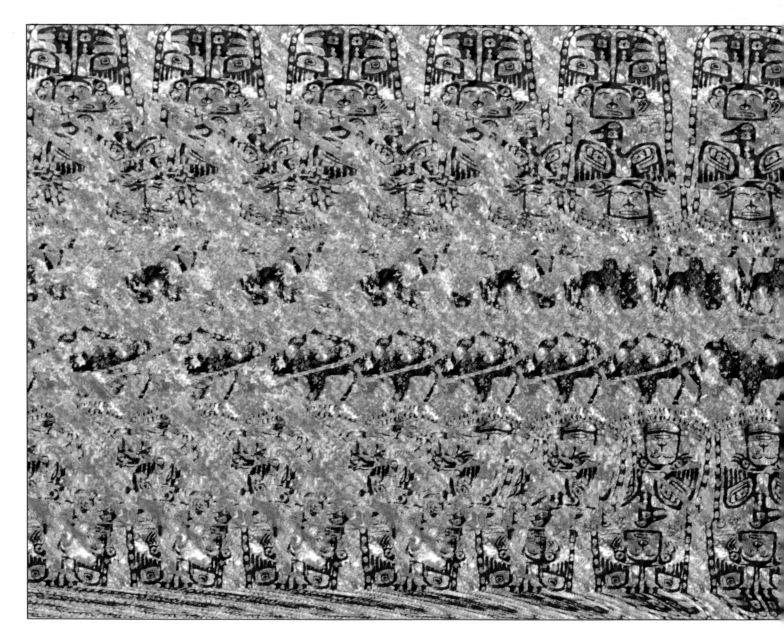

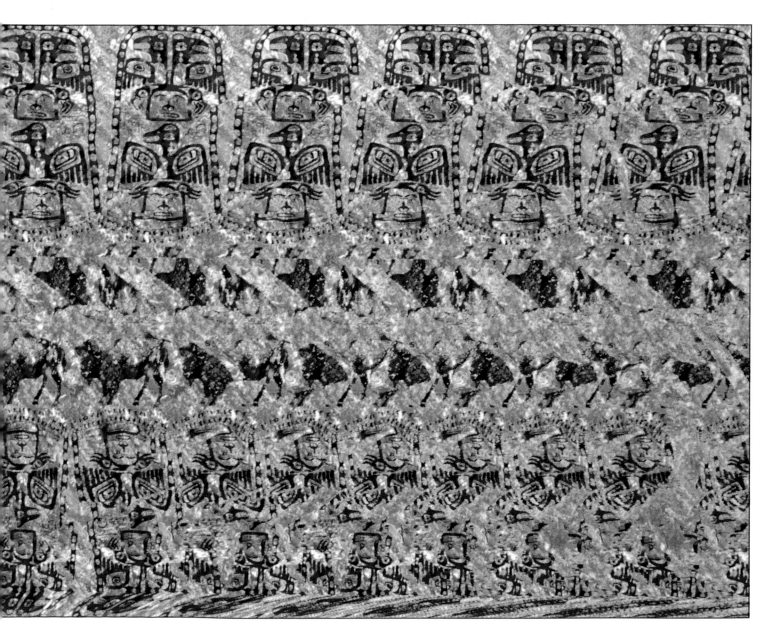

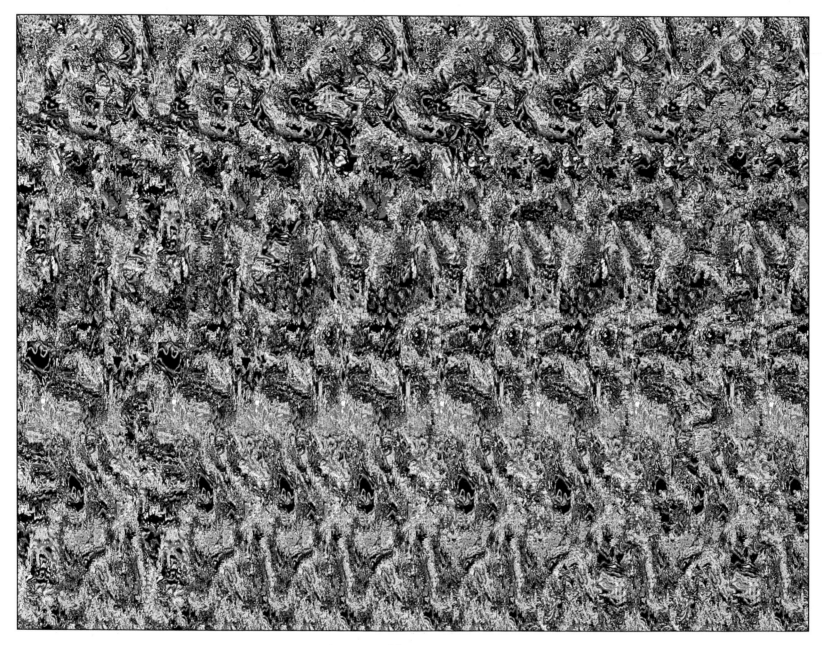

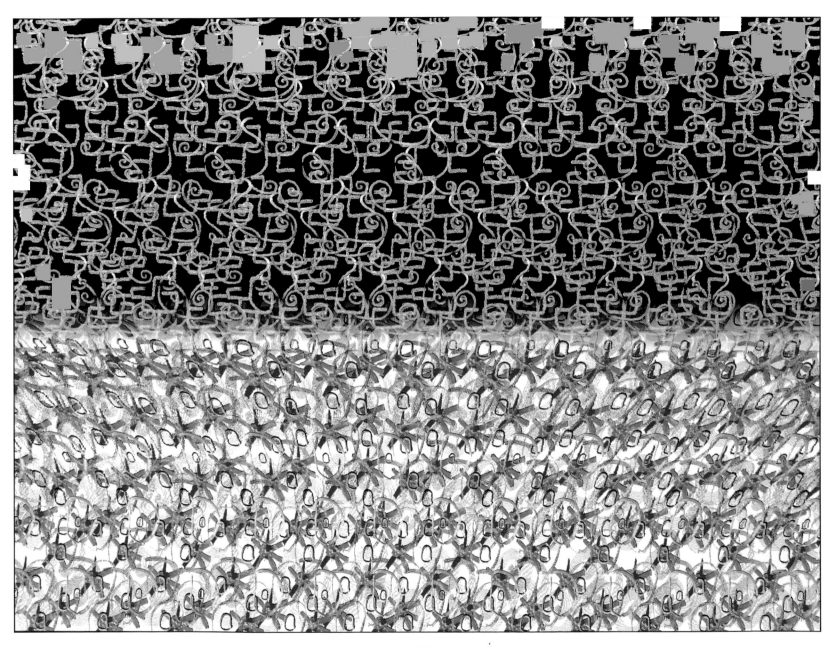

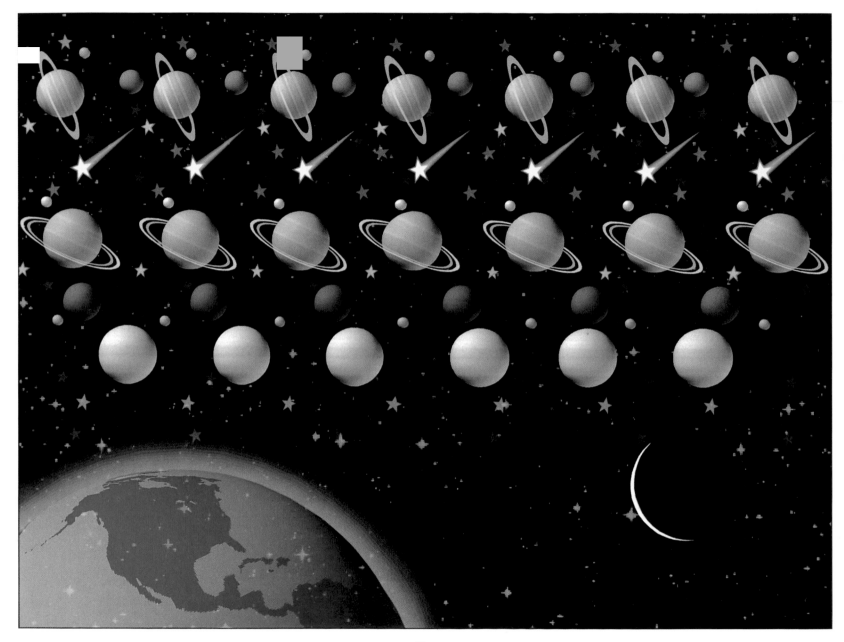

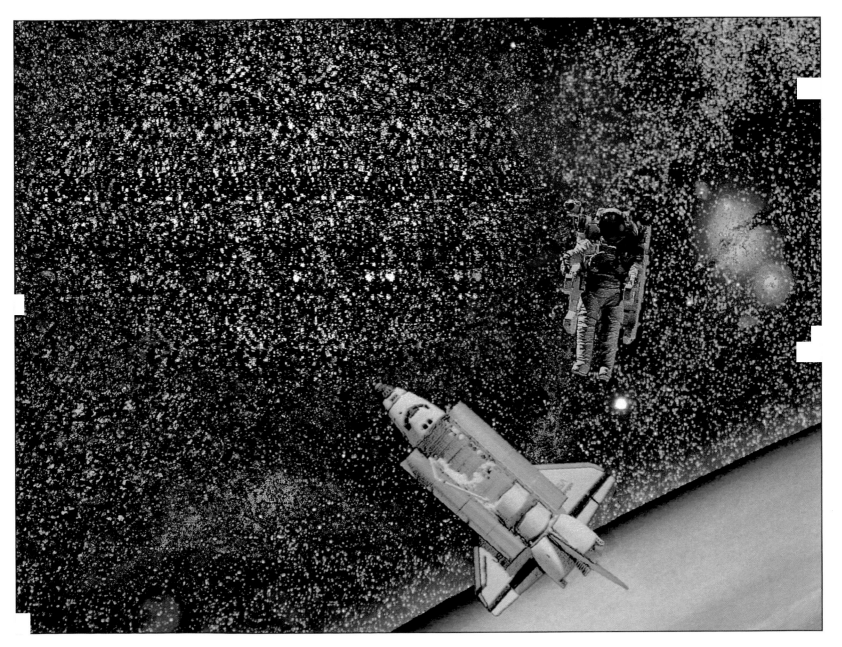

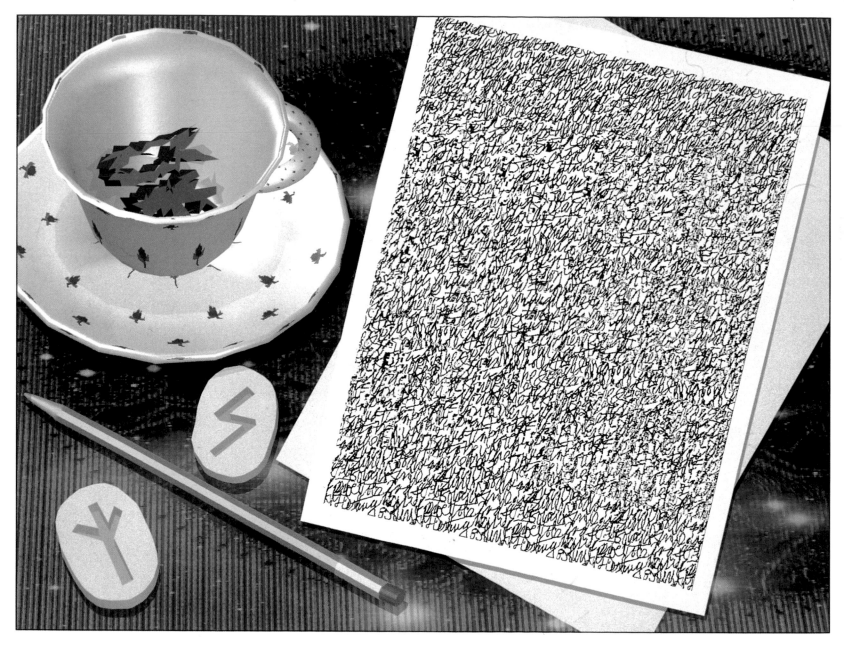

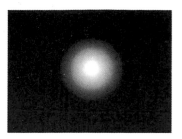

Page 5 Plain Cone

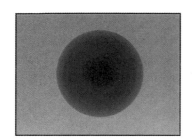

Page 6 Two-Layer Ball

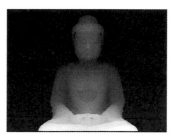

Page 7 Buddha
Page 8 (No Image)

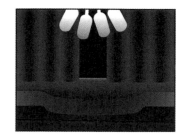

Page 9 Ballerinas

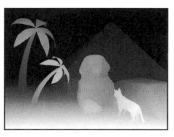

Page 10 Sphinx

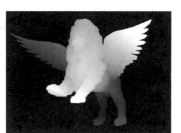

Page 11 Lost Oasis

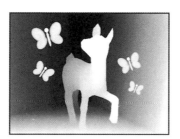

Page 12 Deer

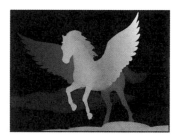

Page 13 Storyland

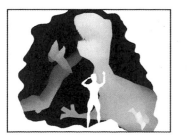

Page 14 Dinner

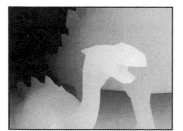

Page 15 Baby Dinosaur

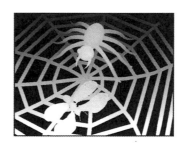

Page 16 Spider and Fly

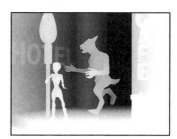

Page 17 Pickup

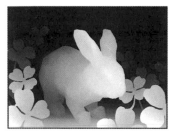

Page 18 Andy's Bunny

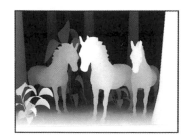

Page 19 Zebras

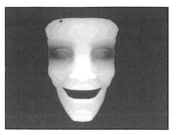

Page 20 Floater Clown

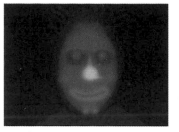

Page 21 Neon Clown

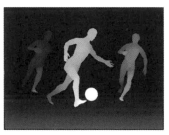

Page 22 Corner Kick

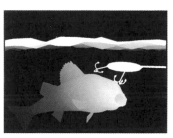

Page 23 Walleye

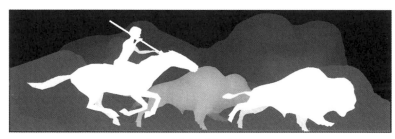

Page 24-25 The Hunt

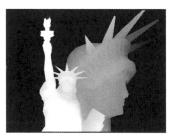

Page 26 Liberty

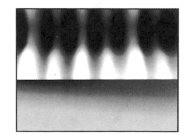

Page 27 Two-Layer, Three-Layer
Page 28 (No Image)

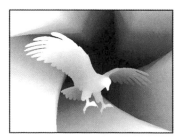

Page 29 The Eagle in Flight

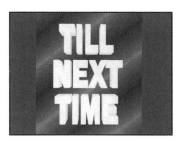

Page 30 Tea Leaves